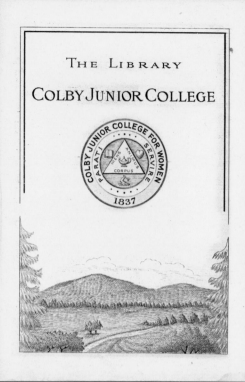

THE BOOK OF BOOKS

IN ART

JUSTUS OF GHENT: *Moses and the Tablets;* Palazzo Barberini, Rome, Italy.

THE
BOOK OF BOOKS
IN ART

A Selection of Biblical Paintings and Sculptures—
Five Centuries of Western Civilization

SELECTED AND EDITED BY

STEPHEN S. KAYSER, PH.D.

Curator, Jewish Museum
Associate Professor of Jewish Art at the
Jewish Theological Seminary
New York

SHENGOLD PUBLISHERS, INC.

NEW YORK · 1956

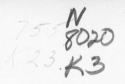

Published by HEMISPHERE PUBLICATIONS, Inc.

Distributed by SHENGOLD PUBLISHERS, Inc.

MANUFACTURED IN THE UNITED STATES OF AMERICA

ACKNOWLEDGEMENTS

We wish to express our sincerest thanks to Dr. Stephen S. Kayser, curator of the Jewish Museum of New York and associate professor of Jewish Art at the Jewish Theological Seminary, for his masterly essay and thoughtful selection of the works represented in this volume; to Mr. Karl Katz, formerly associated with the Metropolitan Museum of Art, for his valuable research assistance and to Evlin Yehoash Dworkin for her technical aid and proof-reading. The following institutions have earned our gratitude for permitting reproduction of masterpieces for use in this book and use of their reference libraries: Library of the Metropolitan Museum of Art, New York; the Frick Reference Library, New York; the New York Public Library; the Library of the Jewish Theological Seminary, New York; the Fogg Art Museum, Harvard University; the National Gallery of Art, Washington, D. C.; the Samuel H. Kress Foundation and The World Publishing Company, Cleveland. We are most grateful to the Jewish Publication Society of America for permission to quote passages from its translation of The Holy Scriptures.

Last, but not least, a word of appreciation to Mr. Ben D. Zevin, President of The World Publishing Company, and Mr. Abe Lerner, its Art Director, for their painstaking efforts in preparing this book for publication.

THE PUBLISHERS

Woodcut based on Michelangelo's *Jeremiah,*
from the Mantua Haggadah, 1568.

CONTENTS

Them hath He filled with wisdom of heart, to work all manner of workmanship, of the craftsman, and of the skilful workman, and of the weaver in colors, in blue, and in purple, in scarlet, and in fine linen, and of the weaver, even of them that do any workmanship, and of those that devise skilful works.

EXODUS 35:35

THE INFLUENCE OF THE OLD
TESTAMENT IN ART

BY STEPHEN S. KAYSER

THE INFLUENCE OF THE OLD

TESTAMENT IN ART

THE BIBLE reached Western civilization through three channels: through the Greek or Latin translations and through verbal teaching, accompanied by images. The themes of the latter show an initial preference for the Old Testament.

Several explanations have been offered for this: first, Christianity spread mainly through the Jewish colonies of the Roman Empire; second, the books of the New Testament were still being edited while the Old Testament in its Greek version was at hand as an established literature of long standing; third, the early Christian teachers employed symbolic imagery to impress their congregants, using Old Testament characters as a guise for new meanings. For instance, Jonah's three days in the whale stood for the resurrection of Christ, which took place three days after his death.

Yet, is it likely that the early Christians invented an array of pictorial Old Testament figures for the purpose of assigning to their stories a different meaning as a symbol for New Testament ideas? It seems much more probable that there was at hand an array of Jewish figural types which the Christians used for their new pictorial interpretations in catacombs, baptisteries, churches, on sarcophagi and in scrolls.

While the Jewish originals are lost, save for a few exceptions like the wall paintings of the Synagogue of Dura Europos of the Common Era, it may be possible some day on the basis of the evidence thus far assembled, and supplemented by future discoveries, to show the step-by-step development of a Jewish pictorial tradition from late antiquity onward, and continuing in the illustrations of medieval manuscripts.

Whereas the Jewish pictorial tradition is scanty and still awaits its historian, the Christian use of Biblical themes in the visual arts unfolds in a practically endless and uninterrupted array of paintings, reliefs, sculptures, etc. From crude beginnings in late antiquity to the glorious heights of what art had to offer during its golden age in the sixteenth and seventeenth centuries—the times of Michelangelo and Rembrandt, and far beyond that—the Bible proved to be a main source of artistic content in Western civilization. The visual arts became greatly responsible for the fact that the herdsmen and heroes of ancient Israel, its priests and prophets, remained alive in the mind of Western man who scarcely realized the remote Oriental origin of these figures, so close had they become to him.

The use of Biblical themes in art, soon after the rather timid beginnings in early Christian times, became the subject of heated theological controversies. In the Eastern Roman Empire they ended in the triumph of the icon, the holy image whose "divine origin," basically unchanged for centuries, thereby impeded any freedom of individual artistic development. The static monumental form of the adored icon precluded the treatment of the vivid Old Testament stories in Byzantine and related art.

In Western Roman Catholicism the attitude toward images was different, the church authorities coming to tolerate them more and more. The attitude of Gregory the Great (circa 600) seems characteristic. He regarded pictures as useful; one should not worship them, but neither should one destroy them. "The picture," he said, "takes the place of reading for the common people. They at least read on the walls what they are unable to read in books."

In Eastern Christendom the Bible picture was dogmatic; in Western Christendom it was conceived as didactic, the main characteristic of Occidental Christian art throughout its history.

This didactic principle liberated the visual arts from the strict pictorial conservatism of the Eastern Orthodox Church and fostered individual trends which soon expressed themselves in the rise of different regional schools of art. Yet the arts under Roman Catholicism were also bound by certain dogmatic doctrines which, as they gradually expanded, developed an entire system for the representation of Biblical themes. It was based on the doctrine, already effective in the catacomb paintings, that the New Testament is contained in the Old, and the Old Testament is fulfilled in the New. This led to what is called "typology" in Christian art, a pictorial parallelism, showing each scene taken from the New Testament, prophetically pre-figured by as many as four scenes from the Old. For fifteen hundred years figures and events from the Old Testament were depicted in Western art according to that principle. They did not tell a story for its own sake but as an anticipation of some specific feature in the life and death of the Christian Savior. If David is shown slaying Goliath, this refers to redemption through the descendant of David, while Goliath represents the forces of sin, paganism, or the Devil himself. There is even an allusion to baptism in this scene: David takes the stones for his sling from a brook (I Samuel, 17:40) which means that salvation comes from the water.

This typological program reached its height when Western art was dominated physically and spiritually by the architecture of the cathedral which was subordinated to theological authority. Statues, reliefs, stained-glass windows, as well as paintings, formed an inseparable unit with the church building. While the stained-glass window by its very nature required the surrounding edifice, the sculptures and paintings of the cathedral still remained aesthetically a part of their original surroundings, even when removed from there.

The big change came when the works of art divorced themselves in form and expression from their setting. Even while still contained within an architectural frame, they became increasingly emancipated from it and assumed the characteristics of self-contained aesthetic units.

This happened first in sculpture. It seems characteristic that the full round human figure was absent in the art of the Byzantine Church, as though there were a fear that it might endeavor to live a life of its own. In the West isolated statues, hermits in stone, attached to the portals of the cathedrals, were held together not as a physical but as a spiritual unit. Gradually, these statues acquired individual *Pl. liv* expressions in the sculpture north of the Alps. Still separated from each other in space, they conversed in looks and in gestures. In Italy their placement in niches gave them a possibility for a life of their own. The niche pro-

[12]

vided the figure with space in which it could move freely. It was an open portal out of which the figure seemed ready to step.

The tendency toward liberation from the dominance of architecture is best shown in the relief. In it the artist overcame any shyness regarding spacial depth and rendered vistas of landscape, and especially architecture, in which the figures were placed at various dis- *Pl. l* tances. The eye of the spectator was drawn into the scene which sought to be accepted not as a part of a wall but as a space of its own. The scientific laws of perspective, first applied in reliefs, enabled the artist to create an independent unit of pictorial representation. The bronze technique favored this type of relief work.

The art of book decoration showed a similar trend. From integration of ornamentation with text it gradually separated the picture from *Pl. lxi* the text, until the illustrating miniatures became landscapes and figure paintings in their own right, independent of their former very close spacial relation to the text.

This liberation was by no means identical with the relinquishing of the typological principle which still remained effective while taking on new guises. But the door was now open for the individual artist to express himself more freely. With the waning power of the cathedral as an aesthetic unit, the work of art was less determined by theological speculation than by the free choice of the artist whose individuality superseded the preponderance of doctrines.

It is interesting to note that as soon as new creative forces were at work, scenes and characters from the Old Testament were conceived more liberally. The dramatic situations characteristic of these scenes needed greater visual realism. While the representations conditioned by the cathedral showed man mainly in his relationship to the "other world," the less doctrinal rendering of Biblical themes stressed more frequently the relationship of man to man. This could be rendered only in natural pictorial surroundings, eschewing the golden background of the foregoing periods which placed man in a metaphysical world and not in real space. Now nature occupied *Pl. xvi, xxiv* the picture more and more and artists came to realize that most of the scenes in the Hebrew Bible—typical of tales which originated in the Near East—called for an outdoor setting.

A painting of a Biblical subject consists of three main elements: color, space and human situation or action. The colors red and blue dominated, as can best be seen in the stained-glass windows. Red was the color of judgment, blue the color of mercy—thus symbolizing the dual roles of Christ as the judge on the one hand and the redeemer on the other. The blue color of the mantle of Mary designates her as the merciful mother. Space in the paintings of the cathedral was determined by the setting of the work itself. Its golden background, endowing the image with light divine, precluded any natural surrounding for the figure. There was little of situation or action, except for the rendering of martyrdom.

With emancipation from the cathedral, the colors in painting became more natural. From the careful rendition of the various hues of surface texture according to certain set standards, the expression of the artist advanced to emotional coloring.

Nature is color in space and atmosphere. Painting is therefore capable of rendering more of the visible world than any other art medium, particularly after the use of oil became prevalent during the sixteenth century. It did not entirely replace the older tempora technique, but it enabled the artist to achieve tones of deep lustre by superimposing several layers of pigment on the canvas or panel. In some instances restorers have found as many as nine coatings of oil in paintings by Titian.

The luminous surface quality of oil prevents

even the best color reproduction from giving the proper impression of the original. (Every reproduction is a subjective interpretation. Photographs of paintings, therefore, are in this sense no different from the engravings of pictures used in the eighteenth century.)

Yet, with all due respect to the magic of color in painting, particularly in the work of the great colorists of the sixteenth and seventeenth centuries, painting does not consist of color alone, but also of spacial composition. The static world of the Eastern church called for the frontality of the figures in the mosaic. Side by side, these figures faced the spectator without individual distinction except for attire and accompanying symbols. Likewise, their creators are not even thought of as artistic individuals. Mosaic, a Greek invention used originally as floor paving, later became the preferred mural technique for walls, as in the art of the Eastern church. Mural painting in *Pl. xxxiii,* Western art continued the preference for the *xxxiv* use of mosaic in files and rows. However, it gradually added a third dimension to the picture-plane in murals. This, too, was an emancipation from the dominance of architecture. True, the mural is adjusted to the space it occupies, but while it is created for a specific setting, it becomes its equal partner and in some cases even takes over the spacial he- *Pl. vi, xiii, xl* gemony. The paintings of Raphael in the Vatican and, especially, Michelangelo's ceil- *Pl. lv–lviii, lx* ing in the Sistine Chapel show the triumph of painting over architecture in the creation of their own space by pictorial means alone.

Murals remained the main category of painting until a change took place in the work of seventeenth century masters like Poussin, whose creations were not devised for any specific setting. Instead, they required framing and it is characteristic that in his self-portrait Poussin showed himself standing alongside empty picture-frames.

In Poussin's paintings the horizon line came down rather low, in contrast to earlier landscape settings. At the same time, the scenery opens into wide vistas. The result is a human calm in the landscape in which figures and *Pl. xx* groups appear in perfect harmony with their surroundings. Human figures and scenery were equal components of the pictorial structure. Neither before nor after Poussin has this complete balance of man and nature been achieved. At times, Poussin interpreted a certain situation from the Biblical text as a portrait of nature itself. The meeting of *Ruth and* *Pl. lx* *Boaz* became a picture of summer. In the work of Poussin's contemporary, Claude Lorrain, figures (which he often did not even paint himself) dwindled to mere *staffage*; while in the transparency of the sky, with filtered sunlight, he introduced new aerial effects. Claude Lorrain's pictorial compositions were held *Pl. xl* together by the side wings of the scenery arrangement, a typical example of the stage character of French landscapes.

National characteristics like this come into focus as soon as the unifying power of the church diminishes. While in French paint- *Pl. xl* ings the spacial setting resembles that of a *lx* stage, the Italians render their space arrangements stereometrically, predicated on the laws *Pl. lx* of perspective and thus enabling figures to move therein with ease. To render these movements convincingly, the Italian masters had *Pl. xl* to look about for models and these they found in the art of antiquity where the well-proportioned human body was shown in a variety of postures which, combined with natural space provided by perspective, led to the final conquest of reality.

In contrast to the unified space of Italian painting, the German masters based their settings more on experience than on scientific study. They divided the picture-plane into *Pl. xl* various sections according to the theme, thereby neglecting distance.

In the treatment of interiors national charac-

[14]

Pl. xlvi teristics were likewise revealed. Wherever the Italians showed an indoor setting, it remained clearly visible and defined, with the exception of a few nocturnal scenes in which an intruding light meant revelation of the Divine Spirit.

Pl. lxviii When painting in northern countries came to a climax in the art of Rembrandt light, growing out of the dark, became an active force which projected the interior into the infinite. In Italian painting the interior was clearly arranged architecture; with Rembrandt, it created a mysterious atmosphere.

Pl. vi, xi, xlix The Italian painter liked to show construction which led to bold vistas in ceiling paintings and to oversized, yet impressive, interiors. Pl. lxv Within these constructions of interiors and exteriors, the Italian artist placed man as Pl. ii master of space. Adam, the first man, became the image of bodily perfection shaped in the image of God. In Michelangelo's Sistine Chapel ceiling, the detail called *Creation of Adam* shows the first man of the Old Covenant in perfect form. He is roused to Pl. i become the image of God through the touch of forefingers. The tragic expression on his face indicates that Adam at the same time anticipates the fate of the first man of the New Covenant.

Contemporary scholars have made it abundantly clear that the ceiling paintings of the Sistine Chapel represent a complete typological compendium which could hardly be otherwise in the chapel of the Pope. For instance, the very shape of Noah's Ark in the scene of Pl. viii the Flood likens the ark to the church, the haven of salvation floating away from doomed, desperate mankind. These underlying meanings in Michelangelo's work were overlooked or misinterpreted for a long time, but there can be no doubt as to their existence. The acceptance of this fact can only contribute to a better understanding of the treatment of the Biblical themes in Western civilization.

While the typology makes the Sistine Chapel an arsenal of symbolical concatenation, the fact also remains that in comparison to the New Testament, the Old had much more prominence in the life work of Michelangelo. His *Moses* became the most famous piece of Pl. xxxvii sculpture in Western civilization. In the minds of millions, the Hebrew leader and prophet is pictured in the form which Michelangelo gave him. And while it may be only a legend that the Jews of Rome made pilgrimages to the church in which the statue was finally placed, the spiritual kinship between the man who met God face to face and the creation of the Italian master remains unquestionable.*

Similarly impressive appears Michelangelo's *Jeremiah*—the traditional author of the Pl. lvi Lamentations—in the Sistine Chapel, whom he depicts mourning over the fall of Jerusalem. The impression which this figure made on the Jews of the sixteenth century is well attested by the fact that a woodcut based on Michelangelo's prophet appears in the Haggadah of Mantua, printed in 1561. Because of the woodcut technique, the figure is reversed. The "Judenhut" has been added.

In these towering prophetic figures, however, notwithstanding the complex of underlying meanings behind their creation, there lives, above all, the individuality of the artist. To look for an artist's personal contributions to his theme becomes a gratifying task. For instance, in Masaccio's painting of Adam and Pl. iii Eve being expelled from the Garden of Eden, a fine distinction is made between the man's covering his face in grief and the woman's outcry—the two gestures of distress. Unquestionably, there is no source for this profoundly

* The rejection by Jewish critics of Michelangelo's *Moses* was due mainly to the common misinterpretation that the figure depicts the sudden wrath of Moses upon seeing the dance around the Golden Calf. Michelangelo's Moses sees nothing of the kind. His face actually reflects the violent emotions which accompany the meeting with the Divine Spirit.

human interpretation other than the artist's own invention.

Pl. xlii
Pl. lv
Pl. xxiii
Each passing period added its own stamp to the stories depicted: the fifteenth century favored youth; the sixteenth, man in his prime and the seventeenth, old age. David (and his female counterpart, Judith, of the Apocrypha) became the favorite figure of a hero. The court Pl. l, lxiv scenes of ancient Israel furnished the artist with a welcome opportunity to show the princely splendor of his own time and clientele. Raphael, who aside from being a painter and architect was also custodian of antiquities, Pl. xiii took occasion to reveal this added function in his Biblical work.

Human follies and failures, pain and passion, were depicted, as well as man's hopes and devotion. The full power of the story of how death came into the world is presented Pl. v in the towering representation of *Cain Slaying Abel,* by Titian. The deeply moving and dramatic moment in the story of Joseph when the cup is discovered in Benjamin's sack is the main feature of Ghiberti's relief. The recon- Pl. xxix ciliation of Joseph and his brethren in the background strikes a concluding chord in this touching story, placed within a quiet all-embracing circular architecture.

The relation of man to man is not the only theme of the Bible. Actually it is but another version of the Bible's basic content, the relation of man to God. This necessitated the inclusion of the supernatural and the miraculous in painting, which had just begun to depict reality, placing Biblical figures in natural surroundings. The conquest of this pictorial space was not easy and artists tended to work with it for quite some time without permitting the supernatural world to intrude too much. Yet the changes in the general concept of the world, like Copernicus' discovery that the earth was not the center of the universe, gradually put an end to the predominance of man in art and gave way to other forces.

In painting, the transition characteristic of this development is to be seen in the work of Tintoretto. In his *The Rain of Manna* (it Pl. xxx must be mentioned that the companion piece of this painting is *The Last Supper*) the artist depicted, in a perfectly natural setting, the miracle defying the laws of nature, with the occupations of everyday life detailed with great attention. Moses in the right foreground gazes into the scene of the miraculous happening, while normal life flows on around him. The miraculous and the natural are merged into perfect harmony by the mastery of Tintoretto's brush.

In the following period of Italian art no individual artist was able to deal with the miracle theme as convincingly as Tintoretto. Polazzo's painting of Elijah rising in a chariot Pl. liii of fire makes one pause and speculate on how this theme might have been handled by a truly great artist. Everything is there—the ecstacy of the companion who shows a great resemblance to Elijah himself (indicating the artist's true understanding of the Biblical narrative) and the cosmic atmosphere in which the miracle takes place. And yet one can see, in the well-studied heads of the horses, for instance, that only good craftsmanship and not true genius was at work here.

Lanfranco's painting *Hagar in the Desert* Pl. xvii may not rank among the great masterpieces, either, yet the way in which it shows young Ishmael under divine protection as expressed in the covering wing of the angel is indicative of the extent to which the touching story of the Bible found an echo in the human sensitivity of the artist.

Before the trend toward pictorial realism impelled Western religious art into humanistic expression, the relation of man to the divine posed no problem. In a world not based on the dictates of space, the heavens could always be close by. Man lived in the immediate vicinity of the divine. It was to become

Rembrandt's main achievement to reverse that relationship in his Biblical paintings and etchings—the divine power moved into the vicinity of man. Rembrandt's Biblical creations are even more remarkable when one considers that Calvinistic Protestantism had no use at all for religious art. According to its doctrine the only true subject of art was the visible world but not the intangible realm of the spirit and faith. There is abundant proof of this attitude in Dutch paintings of the seventeenth century. This change regarding artistic subject matter affected the Hebrew Bible in a manner which can almost be called tragic. On the one hand Protestantism placed new emphasis on the Old Testament; on the other, the Reformers were opposed to artistic treatment of Biblical subjects. Rembrandt's work, to a great extent based on the Bible, was therefore a rare exception which can be explained only by his personal preference for Biblical themes.

To Rembrandt, the Old Testament was not a prefiguration of the New Testament. He treated its various scenes without any visible or hidden typological references, thus carrying out the final emancipation from the church limitations which had governed the arts for one and a half millenia. Protestantism rejected the pictorial typology of the Catholic tradition, but did little in the exploration of the human values of the Old Testament for the sake of the visual arts.

Rembrandt, on the contrary, made them the content of his paintings, etchings and drawings. He approached his themes on a personal basis, which reveals itself in his frequent use of the members of his family, particularly his son Titus, as models. He placed his figures in a setting which, through the use of light, shadow and atmosphere, caused them to appear in an unearthly glow.

Thereby, Rembrandt's Biblical scenes became more and more indicative instead of descriptive. We divine rather than see what is in them. *David Playing before Saul* becomes a drama of great intensity. Who can actually tell to what specific Biblical passage this presentation refers? The painting encompasses, rather, the entire complex relation between David and Saul. Two kings, one fallen from the grace of God, the other just anointed, are shown together and yet each of them is solitary, one playing the harp and the other touching a murderous weapon; one with eyes cast downward while absorbed in musical harmonies, the other, in his dual nature, showing one eye covered and the other open. Art has only a few works to show in which form and content, tension and ease, motion and rest are balanced with such profound feeling. In its human tragedy we sense the guiding hand of divine power.

Pl. xliii

*

In the following selection of Biblical subjects there is a wide range, from Master Bertram's rustic treatment of Isaac's domestic conflicts to the sophisticated rendering of Sarah's surprise in Tiepolo's painting. Both works, however, were created at a time when the integrating forces of an organic style in art were at work.

Pl. xxii

Pl. xvii

Toward the end of the eighteenth century the stylistic lifeblood of art began to be diluted and finally the transfusions of styles borrowed from the past became more and more necessary to keep the arts alive through the nineteenth century. The treatment of Biblical subjects never ceased, but they lacked the air of a style to breathe. In their isolation the arts, for the first time in Western civilization, managed to live without subject matter. Style is not only a matter of form; it is a basic need for artistic communication. Deprived of this general denominator which mediates between the work of art and its consumer, Biblical subjects became more and more sporadic. Only William Blake was strong enough to create a Biblical image as a pictorial world in itself.

The nineteenth century brought the Jewish artists to the fore. The most prominent of them, with the exception of Camille Pissarro, turned to Biblical themes, among others. Only in our own time can we observe a more comprehensive rendering of the Biblical subject in over forty paintings and numerous etchings by Marc Chagall and in the extensive and intensive work of Ben-Zion. These artists prove convincingly that the Bible as a subject has by no means lost its attraction. They are strong individuals who created their own style in the rendering of Biblical themes. To show their significance would necessitate a monographic presentation of their characteristics.

The following selection, while in no way intended to be systematic, seeks to show the various treatments of Biblical subjects during the time when general trends in Western art favored them as an integrated expression not only of individuals but also of the period of their origin.

It seems rather significant that at the time when Biblical criticism became a threat to the authority of the Scriptures, the artistic treatment of Biblical subjects lost its convincing power, sinking to its lowest ebb in the last century's theatrical treatment at the hand of Bible "illustrators" at a time when Biblical criticism was reaching its peak. Not that there was a direct connection between the two phenomena, but they show two expressions of the same underlying *Zeitgeist*.

The following selection shows various treatments of the Biblical theme at a time when the Bible was still an unchallenged factor in Western civilization. The great number of works of art based upon Scripture during that period cannot even be intimated. This impact of the Bible upon the visual arts of Western civilization is liable to pose a rather paradoxical question: how was it possible that the Scriptures—itself seemingly utterly opposed to imagery—could evoke such an endless array of images?

The Biblical ban against imagery is to be understood as mainly directed against idols. The forbidden "graven image" was, of course, the pagan deity of stone or metal. In the uncompromising struggle against the idolatrous art practice of the neighboring peoples of ancient Israel lies, strange as it may seem, the actual reason why the Old Testament could become a main source for subjects in Western art. To understand this, one has to realize that the Biblical prohibition against idolatry and insistence on the worship of one God meant the extinction of all mythological elements in the ancient Hebrew religion. Biblical scholars have tried to show where old Semitic myths still peep through the meshes of the Biblical text. Even if that were so, it would only prove the complete and final victory of the strong anti-mythological trend which became a basic characteristic of Judaism. The Bible tolerates no half-deities. One of the most fantastic errors of nineteenth century Biblical criticism has been to regard the Patriarchs, Moses, Joshua and even the Kings of ancient Israel, as transformations of some local major or minor Semitic deities.

While modern scholarship has finally put these critics in their place, they could have learned the true nature of these metamorphic "deities" from the artists who depicted Biblical figures as humans among humans. Mythology always creates idols. That is exactly what the ancient Hebrews avoided, in the text of the Scriptures as well as in their artistic practice which consisted mainly of erecting a sanctuary to the Deity who tolerated no images, particularly of Himself. While they could not "depict" their stories through visual means, their sacred books became vividly

[18]

descriptive in the general characterization of figures as well as in the many details of which the dramatic and lyric scenes in the text are composed. An artist seeking inspiration need not approach the Scriptures as a scholar. The text immediately tells him, clearly and specifically, what he has to know about an individual or a situation.

For this transformation of the text the arts of that period, from which the ensuing selection is chosen, offered an arsenal of humanistic expressions, the reality of space and atmosphere, the movements of the human body, the natural color scheme and the security of an integrated, organic style.

At the same time as these increased representational possibilities arose, there came to the fore another content, dormant though not forgotten since antiquity, but not shaped as a theme in itself: the gods and heroes, the fables and tales of ancient Greece and Rome. It was as if Shem and Japhet, Jerusalem and Athens, were again to be confronted—the beauty of holiness and the holiness of beauty. Side by side with characters from the Old Testament figures from the mythology of antiquity populated the pictorial realm of Western art. This

time there was no struggle for survival between the two worlds. They were brought to life by the same artistic principles of representation and they co-existed peacefully.

It is even just to say that without a new awareness of the artistic achievement of antiquity, the rendering of the Biblical themes as they are shown in this volume would not have been possible. And yet the Biblical scenes appear to be more vivid, more human, more inspired, compared with the themes taken from ancient mythology and literature.

For this, the antithesis of Judea and Greece seems to be responsible—the Jewish concept of man created in God's image and the Greek creation of its gods in the image of man. The gods of Greece and Rome lost their power, which could never be retrieved, while the God of the Bible remained a reality.

The inspiration which the artists received from the Scriptures is observed with pride by the people of the Bible to this very day, while perfectly aware of the fact that though the Bible is *of* the Jews it is by no means *for* them alone. In religion, in law, in literature, as well as in art, it has become, to quote Goethe, "the Book of all peoples."

[19]

TABLE OF PLATES

[22]

PLATES

And God created man in His own
image . . .

GENESIS 1:27

. . . and man became a living soul.

GENESIS 2:7

· · · ויברא אלהים את־האדם בצלמו
בראשית א׳ כז

· · · ויהי האדם לנפש חיה·
בראשית ב׳ ז

I. MICHELANGELO: *Creation of Man* (DETAIL); Cappella Sistina, Vatican, Rome, Italy.

And when the woman saw that the tree was good for food, and that it was a delight to the eyes, and that the tree was to be desired to make one wise, she took of the fruit thereof, and did eat; and she gave also unto her husband with her, and he did eat.

GENESIS 3:6

ותרא האשה כי טוב העץ למאכל וכי תאוה־הוא לעינים ונחמד העץ להשכיל ותקח מפריו ותאכל ותתן גם־לאישה עמה ויאכל.

בראשית ג׳ ו

II. LUCAS CRANACH (The Elder): *Adam and Eve;* Gemaeldegallerie, Dresden, Germany.

Therefore the Lord God sent him forth
from the Garden of Eden . . .

GENESIS 3:23

וישלחהו ה׳ אלהים מגן־עדן · · ·

בראשית ג׳ כג

III. MASACCIO: *The Expulsion from Paradise;* Cappella Brancacci, Florence, Italy.

. . . And Abel was a keeper of sheep,
but Cain was a tiller of the ground. And
in process of time it came to pass, that
Cain brought of the fruit of the ground
an offering unto the Lord. And Abel,
he also brought of the firstlings of his
flock and of the fat thereof. And the
Lord had respect unto Abel and to his
offering; but unto Cain and to his offering He had not respect. And Cain was
very wroth, and his countenance fell.

GENESIS 4:2-5

· · · ויהי־הבל רעה צאן וקין היה עבד
אדמה·   ויהי מקץ ימים ויבא קין מפרי
האדמה מנחה לה׳· והבל הביא גם־הוא
מבכרות צאנו ומחלבהן וישע ה׳ אל־הבל
ואל־מנחתו·   ואל־קין ואל־מנחתו לא
שעה ויחר לקין מאד ויפלו פניו·
בראשית ד׳ ב־ה

IV. BARTOLOMMEO BELLANO: *Cain and Abel;* Chiesa del Santo, Padua, Italy.

And Cain spoke unto Abel his brother.
And it came to pass, when they were in
the field, that Cain rose up against Abel
his brother, and slew him.

GENESIS 4:8

ויאמר קין אל־הבל אחיו ויהי בהיותם
בשדה ויקם קין אל־הבל אחיו ויהרגהו·
בראשית ד' ח

v. TITIAN: *Cain Slaying Abel;* Chiesa della Salute, Venice, Italy.

And God said unto Noah . . . 'Make thee an ark of gopher wood; . . . And I, behold, I do bring the flood of waters upon the earth, to destroy all flesh, wherein is the breath of life, from under heaven; everything that is in the earth shall perish. But I will establish My covenant with thee; and thou shalt come into the ark, thou, and thy sons, and thy wife, and thy sons' wives with thee.'

GENESIS 6:13–18

ויאמר אלהים לנח · · · · עשה לך תבת
עצי־גפר · · · · ואני הנני מביא את־
המבול מים על־הארץ לשחת כל־בשר
אשר־בו רוח חיים מתחת השמים כל
אשר־בארץ יגוע· והקמתי את־בריתי
אתך ובאת אל־התבה אתה ובניך ואשתך
ונשי־בניך אתך·

בראשית ו' יג־יח

VI. RAPHAEL and GIULIO ROMANO: *Building of the Ark;* Loggia in the Vatican, Rome, Italy.

And of every living thing of all flesh,
two of every sort shalt thou bring into
the ark, to keep them alive with thee;
they shall be male and female. Of the
fowl after their kind, and of the cattle
after their kind ... two of every sort shall
come unto thee, to keep them alive.

GENESIS 6:19–20

ומכל־החי מכל־בשר שנים מכל תביא
אל־התבה להחית אתך זכר ונקבה יהיו·
מהעוף למינהו ומן־הבהמה למינה מכל
רמש האדמה למינהו שנים מכל יבאו
אליך להחיות·

בראשית ו׳ יט־כ

VII. JAN BRUEGHEL: *Noah's Ark;* Nationalmuseum, Budapest, Hungary.

And the flood was forty days upon the earth; . . . And the waters prevailed exceedingly upon the earth; and all the high mountains that were under the whole heaven were covered . . . And all flesh perished that moved upon the earth, both fowl, and cattle, and beast, and every swarming thing that swarmeth upon the earth, and every man; all in whose nostrils was the breath of the spirit of life, whatsoever was in the dry land, died.

GENESIS 7:17–22

ויהי המבול ארבעים יום על־הארץ ··· והמים גברו מאד מאד על־הארץ ויכסו כל־ההרים הגבהים אשר־תחת כל־ השמים ···· ויגוע כל־בשר הרמש על־ הארץ בעוף ובבהמה ובחיה ובכל־השרץ השרץ על־הארץ וכל האדם· כל· אשר נשמת־רוח חיים באפיו מכל אשר בחרבה מתו·

בראשית ז׳ יז־כב

VIII. MICHELANGELO: *The Deluge;* Cappella Sistina, Vatican, Rome, Italy.

And Noah builded an altar unto the Lord; and took of every clean beast, and of every clean fowl, and offered burnt-offerings on the altar.

ויבן נח מזבח לה׳ ויקח מכל הבהמה הטהרה ומכל העוף הטהור ויעל עלת במזבח.

בראשית ח׳ כ

IX. MICHELANGELO: *Noah's Sacrifice;* Cappella Sistina, Vatican, Rome, Italy.

And Ham, the father of Canaan, saw
the nakedness of his father, and told
his two brethren without. And Shem
and Japheth took a garment, and laid it
upon both their shoulders, and went
backward, and covered the nakedness
of their father; and their faces were
backward, and they saw not their father's nakedness.

GENESIS 9:22–23

וירא חם אבי כנען את ערות אביו ויגד
לשני־אחיו בחוץ·   ויקח שם ויפת את־
השמלה וישימו על־שכם שניהם וילכו
אחרנית ויכסו את ערות אביהם ופניהם
אחרנית וערות אביהם לא ראו·
בראשית ט'   כב־כג

x. BERNARDINO LUINI; *Deriding of Noah;* Real Pinacoteca di Brera, Milan, Italy.

And they said: 'Come, let us build us a
city, and a tower, with its top in heaven,
and let us make us a name; lest we be
scattered abroad upon the face of the
whole earth.'

GENESIS 11:4

ויאמרו הבה נבנה־לנו עיר ומגדל וראשו
בשמים ונעשה־לנו שם פן־נפוץ על־פני
כל־הארץ.

בראשית יא׳ ד

XI. BENOZZO GOZZOLI: *The Tower of Babel;* Campo Santo, Pisa, Italy.

And the Lord came down to see the city and the tower, which the children of men builded. And the Lord said: 'Behold, they are one people, and they have all one language; and this is what they begin to do; and now nothing will be withholden from them, which they purpose to do. Come, let us go down, and there confound their language, that they may not understand one another's speech.' So the Lord scattered them abroad from thence upon the face of all the earth; and they left off to build the city. Therefore was the name of it called Babel; because the Lord did there confound the language of all the earth; and from thence did the Lord scatter them abroad upon the face of all the earth.

GENESIS 11:5-9

וירד ה׳ לראת את־העיר ואת־המגדל אשר בנו בני האדם· ויאמר ה׳ הן עם אחד ושפה אחת לכלם וזה החלם לעשות ועתה לא־יבצר מהם כל אשר יזמו לעשות· הבה נרדה ונבלה שם שפתם אשר לא ישמעו איש שפת רעהו· ויפץ ה׳ אתם משם על־פני כל־הארץ ויחדלו לבנת העיר· על־כן קרא שמה בבל כי־ שם בלל ה׳ שפת כל־הארץ ומשם הפיצם ה׳ על־פני כל הארץ·

בראשית יא׳ ה־ט

XII. PIETER BRUEGHEL (The Elder): *The Tower of Babel;* Collection of D. S. Von Beuningen, Rotterdam, Holland.

And Melchizedek king of Salem brought
forth bread and wine; and he was priest
of God the Most High. And he blessed
him, and said: 'Blessed be Abram of
God Most High, Maker of heaven and
earth; and blessed be God the Most
High, who hath delivered thine enemies
into thy hand.' And he gave him a
tenth of all.

GENESIS 14:18–20

ומלכי־צדק מלך שלם הוציא לחם ויין
והוא כהן לאל עליון·   ויברכהו ויאמר
ברוך אברם לאל עליון קנה שמים וארץ·
וברוך אל עליון אשר־מגן צריך בידך
ויתן־לו מעשר מכל·
בראשית יד׳ יח־כ

XIII. RAPHAEL and GIULIO ROMANO: *Abraham Offering Tithes to the King of Salem;*
Loggia in the Vatican, Rome, Italy.

And when the morning arose, then the angels hastened Lot, saying: 'Arise, take thy wife, and thy two daughters that are here; lest thou be swept away in the iniquity of the city.' But he lingered; and the men laid hold upon his hand, and upon the hand of his wife, and upon the hand of his two daughters; the Lord being merciful unto him. And they brought him forth, and set him without the city . . . But his wife looked back from behind him, and she became a pillar of salt.

GENESIS 19:15-16, 26

וכמו השחר עלה ויאיצו המלאכים בלוט
לאמר קום קח את־אשתך ואת־שתי
בנתיך הנמצאת פן־תספה בעון העיר·
ויתמהמה ויחזיקו האנשים בידו וביד־
אשתו וביד שתי בנתיו בחמלת ה׳ עליו
ויצאהו וינחהו מחוץ לעיר · · · ותבט
אשתו מאחריו ותהי נציב מלח·
בראשית יט׳ טו־טז, כו

XIV. ALBRECHT DÜRER: *Flight of Lot;* National Gallery of Art, Washington, D. C., U. S. A.

And Lot went up out of Zoar, and
dwelt in the mountain, and his two
daughters with him; for he feared to
dwell in Zoar; and he dwelt in a cave,
he and his two daughters.

GENESIS 19:30

ויעל לוט מצוער וישב בהר ושתי בנתיו

עמו כי ירא לשבת בצוער וישב במערה

הוא ושתי בנתיו·

בראשית יט׳ ל

xv. FRANS FRANCKEN (The Third): *Lot and His Daughters.*

. . . and he lifted up his eyes and looked,
and, lo, three men stood over against
him; and when he saw them, he ran to
meet them from the tent door . . .
GENESIS 18:2

וישא עיניו וירא והנה שלשה אנשים
נצבים עליו וירא וירץ לקראתם מפתח
האהל · · ·

בראשית יח׳ בְ

XVI. HANS BOL: *Abraham and the Three Angels;* Gemaeldegallerie, Dresden, Germany.

And He said: 'I will certainly return
unto thee when the season cometh
round; and, lo, Sarah thy wife shall
have a son.' And Sarah heard in the
tent door, which was behind him.

GENESIS 18:10

ויאמר שוב אשוב אליך כעת חיה והנה־
בן לשרה אשתך ושרה שמעת פתח האהל
והוא אחריו.

בראשית יח׳ י

xvii. GIOVANNI BATTISTA TIEPOLO: *Sarah Overhears the Angel;* Palazzo Arcivescovile, Udine, Italy.

. . . and the angel of God called to Hagar
out of heaven, and said unto her: 'What
aileth thee, Hagar? fear not; for God
hath heard the voice of the lad where
he is. Arise, lift up the lad, and hold
him fast by thy hand; for I will make
him a great nation.'

GENESIS 21:17–18

· · · · ויקרא מלאך אלהים אל־הגר מן־
השמים ויאמר לה מה־לך הגר אל־תיראי
כי־שמע אלהים אל־קול הנער באשר
הוא־שם·   קומי שאי את־הנער והחזיקי
את־ידך·בו כי־לגוי גדול אשימנו·
בראשית כא׳ יז־יח

XVIII. GIOVANNI LANFRANCO: *Hagar in the Desert;* Louvre, Paris, France.

And they came to the place which God
had told him of; and Abraham built the
altar there, and laid the wood in order,
and bound Isaac his son, and laid him
on the altar, upon the wood. And
Abraham stretched forth his hand, and
took the knife to slay his son.

GENESIS 22:9-10

ויבאו אל־המקום אשר אמר־לו האלהים
ויבן שם אברהם את־המזבח ויערך את־
העצים ויעקד את־יצחק בנו וישם אתו
על־המזבח ממעל לעצים· וישלח אברהם
את־ידו ויקח את־המאכלת לשחט את־
בנו·

בראשית כב' ט־י

XIX. ANDREA DEL SARTO: *Sacrifice of Isaac;* formerly Gemaeldegallerie, Dresden, Germany.

And the angel of the Lord called unto
him out of heaven and said: 'Abraham,
Abraham.' And he said: 'Here am I.'
And he said: 'Lay not thy hand upon
the lad, neither do thou any thing unto
him; for now I know that thou art a
God-fearing man, seeing thou hast not
withheld thy son, thine only son, from
Me.'

GENESIS 22:11–12

ויקרא אליו מלאך ה׳ מן־השמים ויאמר
אברהם אברהם ויאמר הנני· ויאמר
אל־תשלח ידך אל־הנער ואל־תעש לו
מאומה כי עתה ידעתי כי־ירא אלהים
אתה ולא חשכת את־בנך את־יחידך
ממני·

בראשית כב׳ יא־יב

xx. LORENZO GHIBERTI: *Sacrifice of Isaac;* Battistero, Florence, Italy.

Behold, I stand by the fountain of
water; and the daughters of the men
of the city come out to draw water. So
let it come to pass, that the damsel to
whom I shall say: Let down thy pitcher,
I pray thee, that I may drink; and she
shall say: Drink, and I will give thy
camels drink also; let the same be she
that Thou hast appointed for Thy servant, even for Isaac; . . . and it came to
pass, before he had done speaking, that,
behold, Rebecca came out . . . And the
damsel was very fair to look upon . . .

GENESIS 24:13–16

הנה אנכי נצב על־עין המים ובנות אנשי
העיר יצאת לשאב מים·   והיה הנער
אשר אמר אליה הטי־נא כדך ואשתה
ואמרה שתה וגם־גמליך אשקה אתה
הכחת לעבדך ליצחק · · · · ויהי־הוא
טרם כלה לדבר והנה רבקה יצאת · · · ·
והנער טבת מראה מאד·
בראשית כד' יג־טז

XXI. NICOLAS POUSSIN: *Eliezer and Rebecca;* Louvre, Paris, France.

And it came to pass, that when Isaac
was old, and his eyes were dim, so that
he could not see, he called Esau his
elder son, and said unto him: '. . . Behold now, I am old, I know not the day
of my death. Now therefore take, I pray
thee, thy weapons, thy quiver and thy
bow, and go out to the field, and take
me venison; and make me savory food,
such as I love, and bring it to me, that I
may eat; that my soul may bless thee
before I die.' And Rebecca heard when
Isaac spoke to Esau his son.

GENESIS 27:1–5

ויהי כי־זקן יצחק ותכהין עיניו מראת
ויקרא את־עשו בנו הגדל ויאמר אליו
· · · · הנה־נא זקנתי לא ידעתי יום
מותי· ועתה שא־נא כליך תליך וקשתך
וצא השדה וצודה לי צידה· ועשה־לי
מטעמים כאשר אהבתי והביאה לי
ואכלה בעבור תברכך נפשי בטרם אמות·
ורבקה שמעת בדבר יצחק אל־עשו בנו·
בראשית כז' א־ה

XXII. MASTER BERTRAM VAN BYRDE: *Isaac and Esau;* Kunsthalle, Hamburg, Germany.

And he came unto his father, and said:
'My father'; and he said: 'Here am I;
who art thou, my son?' And Jacob said
unto his father: 'I am Esau thy first-
born; I have done according as thou
badest me. Arise, I pray thee, sit and
eat of my venison, that thy soul may
bless me.'

GENESIS 27:18–19

ויבא אל־אביו ויאמר אבי ויאמר הנני
מי אתה בני· ויאמר יעקב אל־אביו
אנכי עשו בכרך עשיתי כאשר דברת אלי
קום־נא שבה ואכלה מצידי בעבור
תברכני נפשך·
בראשית כז׳ יח־יט

XXIII. BERNARDO STROZZI: *Isaac and Jacob;* Museo Civico, Pisa, Italy.

And he dreamed, and behold a ladder
set up on the earth, and the top of it
reached to heaven; and behold the
angels of God ascending and descend-
ing on it.

GENESIS 28:12

ויחלם והנה סלם מצב ארצה וראשו
מגיע השמימה והנה מלאכי אלהים
עלים וירדים בו.

בראשית כח׳ יב

xxiv. HANS BOL: *Jacob's Dream;* Gemaeldegallerie, Dresden, Germany.

Now Rachel had taken the teraphim,
and put them in the saddle of the camel,
and sat upon them. And Laban felt
about all the tent, but found them not.
GENESIS 31:34

ורחל לקחה את־התרפים ותשמם בכר
הגמל ותשב עליהם וימשש לבן את־כל־
האהל ולא מצא·

בראשית לא׳ לד

xxv. SEBASTIEN BOURDON: *Laban Searches for His Idols;* Louvre, Paris, France.

And Joseph dreamed a dream, and he told it to his brethren; '. . . behold, we were binding sheaves in the field, and, lo, my sheaf arose, and also stood upright; and, behold, your sheaves came round about, and bowed down to my sheaf.' . . . And he dreamed yet another dream, and told it to his brethren, and said: 'Behold, I have dreamed yet a dream: and, behold, the sun and the moon and eleven stars bowed down to me.'

GENESIS 37:5-9

ויחלם יוסף חלום ויגד לאחיו · · · ·
והנה אנחנו מאלמים אלמים בתוך
השדה והנה קמה אלמתי וגם־נצבה
והנה תסבינה אלמתיכם ותשתחוין
לאלמתי · · · · ויחלם עוד חלום אחר
ויספר אתו לאחיו ויאמר הנה חלמתי
חלום עוד והנה השמש והירח ואחד עשר
כוכבים משתחוים לי·
בראשית לז׳ ה־ט

XXVI. PERINO DEL VAGA: *Joseph Telling His Dream;* Albertina, Vienna, Austria.

And there passed by Midianites, mer-
chantmen; and they drew and lifted up
Joseph out of the pit, and sold Joseph to
the Ishmaelites for twenty shekels of
silver . . .

GENESIS 37:28

ויעברו אנשים מדינים סחרים וימשכו
ויעלו את־יוסף מן־הבור וימכרו את־
יוסף לישמעאלים בעשרים כסף.
בראשית לז' כח

XXVII. PEDRO DE MOYA: *Joseph Sold by His Brothers;* Prado Museum, Madrid, Spain.

And it came to pass on a certain day, when he went into the house to do his work, and there was none of the men of the house there within, that she caught him by his garment, saying: 'Lie with me.' And he left his garment in her hand, and fled, and got him out.

GENESIS 39:11-12

ויהי כהיום הזה ויבא הביתה לעשות
מלאכתו ואין איש מאנשי הבית שם
בבית· ותתפשהו בבגדו לאמר שכבה
עמי ויעזב בגדו בידה וינס ויצא החוצה·
בראשית לט' יא־יב

XXVIII. GREGORIO LAZZARINI: *Joseph and Potiphar's Wife;* Museo Civico, Verona, Italy.

Then they hastened, and took down
every man his sack to the ground, and
opened every man his sack. And he
searched, beginning at the eldest, and
leaving off at the youngest; and the
goblet was found in Benjamin's sack.

GENESIS 44:11-12

וימהרו ויורדו איש את־אמתחתו ארצה
ויפתחו איש אמתחתו ·   ויחפש בגדול
החל ובקטן כלה וימצא הגביע באמתחת
בנימן ·

בראשית מד׳ יא־יב

xxix. LORENZO GHIBERTI: *The Story of Joseph and His Brothers;* Battistero, Florence, Italy.

And the daughter of Pharaoh came
down to bathe in the river; and her
maidens walked along by the riverside;
and she saw the ark among the flags, and
sent her handmaid to fetch it. And she
opened it, and saw it, even the child;
and behold a boy that wept . . . And
she called his name Moses, and said:
'Because I drew him out of the water.'

EXODUS 2:5-6, 10

ותרד בת־פרעה לרחץ על־היאר ונערתיה
הלכת על־יד היאר ותרא את־התבה
בתוך הסוף ותשלח את־אמתה ותקחה ׃
ותפתח ותראהו את־הילד והנה־נער
בכה ׃ ׃ ׃ ׃ ותקרא שמו משה ותאמר
כי מן־המים משיתהו ׃

שמות ב׳ ה־ו, י

xxx. After RUBENS: *The Finding of Moses* (TAPESTRY); Jewish Museum, New York, N. Y., U. S. A.

. . . And Moses hid his face; for he was
afraid to look upon God.

EXODUS 3:6

ויסתר משה פניו כי ירא מהביט אל־
האלהים·

שמות ג׳ ו

XXXI. RAPHAEL: *Moses before the Burning Bush;* Museo Nazionale, Naples, Italy.

And thus shall ye eat it: with your loins
girded, your shoes on your feet, and
your staff in your hand; and ye shall
eat it in haste—it is the Lord's passover.

EXODUS 12:11

וככה תאכלו אתו מתניכם חגרים נעליכם
ברגליכם ומקלכם בידכם ואכלתם אתו
בחפזון פסח הוא לה׳.

שמות יב׳ יא

XXXII. DIRK BOUTS: *The Passover Meal;* Eglise de St. Pierre, Louvain, Belgium.

And the children of Israel went into the
midst of the sea upon the dry ground;
and the waters were a wall unto them
on their right hand, and on their left.
And the Egyptians pursued, and went
in after them into the midst of the sea,
all Pharaoh's horses, his chariots, and
his horsemen.

EXODUS 14:22-23

ויבאו בני־ישראל בתוך הים ביבשה
והמים להם הומה מימינם ומשמאלם.
וירדפו מצרים ויבאו אחריהם כל סוס
פרעה רכבו ופרשיו אל־תוך הים.
שמות יד' כב־כג

XXXIII. PIERO DI COSIMO: *The Drowning of the Egyptians;* Cappella Sistina, Vatican, Rome, Italy.

And Miriam the prophetess, the sister
of Aaron, took a timbrel in her hand;
and all the women went out after her
with timbrels and with dances.

EXODUS 15:20

ותקח מרים הנביאה אחות אהרן את־
התף בידה ותצאן כל־הנשים אחריה
בתפים ובמחלת·

שמות טו' כ

XXXIV. Attributed to LORENZO COSTA: *Song of Miriam;* National Gallery, London, England.

And when the layer of dew was gone
up, behold upon the face of the wilderness a fine, scale-like thing, fine as the
hoar-frost on the ground. And when
the children of Israel saw it, they said
one to another: 'What is it?'—for they
knew not what it was. And Moses
said unto them: 'It is the bread which
the Lord hath given you to eat.'

EXODUS 16:14-15

ותעל שכבת הטל והנה על־פני המדבר
דק מחספס דק ככפר על־הארץ· ויראו
בני־ישראל ויאמרו איש אל־אחיו מן
הוא כי לא ידעו מה־הוא ויאמר משה
אלהם הוא הלחם אשר נתן ה' לכם
לאכלה·

שמות טז' יד־טו

xxxv. TINTORETTO: *The Rain of Manna;* Chiesa de San Giorgio Maggiore, Venice, Italy.

'Behold, I will stand before thee there upon the rock in Horeb; and thou shalt smite the rock, and there shall come water out of it, that the people may drink.' And Moses did so in the sight of the elders of Israel.

EXODUS 17:6

הנני עמד לפניך שם על־הצור בחרב
והכית בצור ויצאו ממנו מים ושתה העם
ויעש כן משה לעיני זקני ישראל·
שמות יז׳ ו

XXXVI. JACOPO BASSANO: *Israelites Drawing Water from the Rock.*

And Moses turned, and went down
from the mount, with the two tables of
the testimony in his hand; tables that
were written on both their sides; on the
one side and on the other were they
written. And the tables were the work
of God, and the writing was the writing
of God, graven upon the tables.

EXODUS 32:15-16

ויפן וירד משה מן־ההר ושני לחת העדת
בידו לחת כתבים משני עבריהם מזה
ומזה הם כתבים· והלחת מעשה אלהים
המה והמכתב מכתב אלהים הוא חרות
על־הלחת·

שמות לב׳ טו־טז

XXXVII. MICHELANGELO: *Moses;* Chiesa di San Pietro in Vincoli, Rome, Italy.

And it came to pass, as soon as he came
nigh unto the camp, that he saw the
calf and the dancing; and Moses' anger
waxed hot, and he cast the tables out of
his hands, and broke them beneath the
mount.

EXODUS 32:19

ויהי כאשר קרב אל־המחנה וירא את־
העגל ומחלת ויחר־אף משה וישלך מידו
את־הלחת וישבר אתם תחת ההר.
שמות לב׳ יט

xxxviii. TINTORETTO: *Worship of the Golden Calf* (detail); Chiesa di Santa Maria dell' Orto, Venice, Italy.

And they took of the fruit of the land in
their hands, and brought it down unto
us, and brought us back word, and
said: 'Good is the land which the Lord
our God giveth unto us.'

ויקחו בידם מפרי הארץ ויורדו אלינו
וישבו אתנו דבר ויאמרו טובה הארץ
אשר־ה׳ אלהינו נתן לנו.
דברים א׳ כה

XXXIX. NICOLAS POUSSIN: *Fruit of the Promised Land;* Louvre, Paris, France.

Then spoke Joshua to the Lord . . . and
he said in the sight of Israel: 'Sun, stand
thou still upon Gibeon; and thou,
Moon, in the valley of Aijalon.' And
the sun stood still, and the moon stayed,
until the nation had avenged themselves
of their enemies . . .

JOSHUA 10:12–13

אז ידבר יהושע לה׳ · · · · ויאמר לעיני
ישראל שמש בגבעון דום וירח בעמק
אילון· וידם השמש וירח עמד עד־יקם
גוי איביו·

יהושע י׳ יב־יג

XL. RAPHAEL and RAPHAELINO DEL COLLE: *Joshua Holds back the Sun;* Loggia in the
Vatican, Rome, Italy.

Then went Samson down . . . and, behold, a young lion roared against him.
And the spirit of the Lord came mightily upon him, and he rent him as one
would have rent a kid . . .

JUDGES 14:5-6

וירד שמשון · · · · והנה כפיר אריות
שאג לקראתו· ותצלח עליו רוח ה׳
וישסעהו כשסע הגדי·
שופטים יד׳ ה־ו

XLI. ALBRECHT DÜRER: *Samson and the Lion* (WOODCUT); Metropolitan Museum of Art, New York, N. Y., U. S. A.

Then Samuel took the horn of oil, and anointed him in the midst of his brethren; and the spirit of the Lord came mightily upon David from that day forward . . .

FIRST SAMUEL 16:13

ויקח שמואל את־קרן השמן וימשח אתו
בקרב אחיו ותצלח רוח־ה׳ אל־דוד
מהיום ההוא.

שמואל א, טז׳ יג

XLII. CLAUDE LORRAIN: *Samuel Anointing David;* Louvre, Paris, France.

And it came to pass, when the spirit from God was upon Saul, that David took the harp, and played with his hand; so Saul found relief, and it was well with him, and the evil spirit departed from him.

FIRST SAMUEL 16:23

והיה בהיות רוח־אלהים אל־שאול ולקח
דוד את־הכנור ונגן בידו ורוח לשאול
וטוב לו וסרה מעליו רוח הרעה·
שמואל א, טז׳ כג

XLIII. REMBRANDT: *David Playing before Saul;* Mauritshuis, The Hague, Holland.

And David ran, and stood over the
Philistine, and took his sword, and
drew it out of the sheath thereof, and
slew him, and cut off his head there-
with . . .

FIRST SAMUEL 17:51

וירץ דוד ויעמד אל הפלשתי ויקח את־
חרבו וישלפה מתערה וימתתהו ויכרת־
בה את־ראשו.

שמואל א, יז׳ נא

XLIV. ANDREA DEL VERROCCHIO: *David with Goliath's Head;* Museo Nazionale, Florence, Italy.

And it came to pass at eventide, that David arose from his bed, and walked upon the roof of the king's house; and from the roof he saw a woman bathing; and the woman was very beautiful to look upon. And David sent and inquired after the woman. And one said: 'Is not this Bathsheba, the daughter of Eliam, the wife of Uriah the Hittite?'

SECOND SAMUEL 11:2-3

ויהי לעת הערב ויקם דוד מעל משכבו ויתהלך על־גג בית־המלך וירא אשה רחצת מעל הגג והאשה טובת מראה מאד· וישלח דוד וידרש לאשה ויאמר הלוא־זאת בת־שבע בת־אליעם אשת אוריה החתי·

שמואל ב, יא׳ ב־ג

xLV. LUCAS CRANACH (The Elder): *David and Bathsheba;* Kaiser Friedrich Museum, Berlin, Germany.

And Abigail came to Nabal; and, behold, he held a feast in his house, like
the feast of a king; and Nabal's heart
was merry within him, for he was very
drunken . . .

FIRST SAMUEL 25:36

ותבא אביגיל אל־נבל והנה־לו משתה
בביתו כמשתה המלך ולב נבל טוב·עליו
והוא שכר עד־מאד·

שמואל א, כה׳ לו

XLVI. GIOVANNI BATTISTA TIEPOLO: *Nabal Dining with Abigail;* Museo Civico Correr, .
Venice, Italy.

And the king said: 'Divide the living child in two, and give half to the one, and half to the other.' Then spoke the woman whose the living child was unto the king, for her heart yearned upon her son, and she said: 'Oh, my lord, give her the living child, and in no wise slay it.' . . . Then the king answered and said: 'Give her the living child, and in no wise slay it: she is the mother thereof.'

FIRST KINGS 3:25-27

ויאמר המלך גזרו את־הילד החי לשנים
ותנו את־החצי לאחת ואת־החצי לאחת׃
ותאמר האשה אשר־בנה החי אל־המלך
כי־נכמרו רחמיה על־בנה ותאמר בי
אדני תנו־לה את־הילוד החי והמת אל־
תמיתהו ‏ ‏ ‏ ‏ ויען המלך ויאמר תנו־
לה את־הילוד החי והמת לא תמיתהו
היא אמו׃

מלכים א, ג׳ כה־כז

XLVII. GIORGIONE: *The Judgment of Solomon;* Galleria Uffizi, Florence, Italy.

But the other said: 'It shall be neither
mine nor thine; divide it.'
FIRST KINGS 3:26

וזאת אמרת גם־לי גם־לך לא יהיה
גזרו. . .
מלכים א, ג' כו

XLVIII. NICOLAS POUSSIN: *The Judgment of Solomon;* Louvre, Paris, France.

And it came to pass in the four hundred
and eightieth year after the children of
Israel were come out of the land of
Egypt, in the fourth year of Solomon's
reign over Israel, in the month Ziv,
which is the second month, that he began to build the house of the Lord.

FIRST KINGS 6:1

ויהי בשמונים שנה וארבע מאות שנה
לצאת בני־ישראל מארץ־מצרים בשנה
הרביעית בחדש זו הוא החדש השני
למלך שלמה על־ישראל ויבן הבית לה׳.
מלכים א, ו׳ א

XLIX. FRANCESCO PESELLINO (?): *The Building of the Temple;* Fogg Museum of Art, Harvard University, Cambridge, Mass., U. S. A.

And when the Queen of Sheba heard
of the fame of Solomon because of the
name of the Lord, she came to prove
him with hard questions. And she came
to Jerusalem with a very great train,
with camels that bore spices and gold
very much, and precious stones; and
when she was come to Solomon, she
spoke with him of all that was in her
heart.

FIRST KINGS 10:1-2

ומלכת־שבא שמעת את־שמע שלמה לשם
ה׳ ותבא לנסתו בחידות׃ ותבא ירושלמה
בחיל כבד מאד גמלים נשאים בשמים
וזהב רב־מאד ואבן יקרה ותבא אל־
שלמה ותדבר אליו את כל־אשר היה עם־
לבבה׃

מלכים א, י׳ א־ב

L. LORENZO GHIBERTI: *Solomon and the Queen of Sheba;* Battistero, Florence, Italy.

And Solomon told her all her questions;
there was not any thing hid from the
king which he told her not.

FIRST KINGS 10:3

ויגד־לה שלמה את־כל־דבריה לא־היה
דבר נעלם מן־המלך אשר לא הגיד לה׃
מלכים א, י׳ ג

LI. PIERO DELLA FRANCESCA: *Solomon and the Queen of Sheba;* Duomo, Arezzo, Italy.

And she said: 'As the Lord thy God
liveth, I have not a cake, only a handful
of meal in the jar, and a little oil in the
cruse; and, behold, I am gathering two
sticks, that I may go in and dress it for
me and my son, that we may eat it, and
die.' And Elijah said unto her: 'Fear not
. . . For thus saith the Lord, the God of
Israel: The jar of meal shall not be
spent, neither shall the cruse of oil fail,
until the day that the Lord sendeth rain
upon the land.'

FIRST KINGS 17:12–14

ותאמר חי־ה׳ אלהיך אם־יש־לי מעוג כי
אם־מלא כף־קמח בכד ומעט־שמן
בצפחת והנני מקששת שנים עצים ובאתי
ועשיתיהו לי ולבני ואכלנהו ומתנו·
ויאמר אליה אליהו אל־תיראי · · · כי
כה אמר ה׳ אלהי ישראל כד הקמח לא
תכלה וצפחת השמן לא תחסר עד יום
תתן־ה׳ גשם על־פני האדמה·
מלכים א, יז׳ יב־יד

LII. JAN MASSYS: *Elijah and the Widow of Sarepta;* Kunsthalle, Karlsruhe, Germany.

. . . behold, there appeared a chariot of
fire, and horses of fire, which parted
them both asunder; and Elijah went up
by a whirlwind into heaven.

SECOND KINGS 2:11

· · · והנה רכב־אש וסוסי אש ויפרדו
בין שניהם ויעל אליהו בסערה השמים·
מלכים ב, ב׳ יא

LIII. FRANCESCO POLAZZO: *Elijah Taken up in a Chariot of Fire;* Samuel H. Kress Collection, New York, N. Y., U. S. A.

. . . He spoke by the hand of all His
servants the prophets . . .

SECOND KINGS 17:23

··· כאשר דבר ביד כל־עבדיו הנביאים ···
מלכים ב, יז׳ כג

LIV. By an unknown master: *A Prophet;* Eglise de Saint Pierre, Avignon, France.

The Lord God hath given me
The tongue of them that are taught,
That I should know how to sustain with
words him that is weary . . .
ISAIAH 50:4

אדני ה׳ נתן לי לשון למודים לדעת
לעות את־יעף דבר · · ·
ישעיה נ׳ ד

ᴸⱽ. MICHELANGELO: *The Prophet Isaiah;* Cappella Sistina, Vatican, Rome, Italy.

The word that came to Jeremiah from
the Lord, saying: Stand in the gate of
the Lord's house, and proclaim there
this word, and say: Hear the word of
the Lord . . . : Amend your ways and
your doings, and I will cause you to
dwell in this place.

JEREMIAH 7:1-3

הדבר אשר־היה אל־ירמיהו מאת ה׳
לאמר· עמד בשער בית ה׳ וקראת שם
את־הדבר הזה ואמרת שמעו דבר ה׳·····
היטיבו דרכיכם ומעלליכם ואשכנה
אתכם במקום הזה·

ירמיה ז׳ א־ג

HIEREMIAS

LVI. MICHELANGELO: *The Prophet Jeremiah;* Cappella Sistina, Vatican, Rome, Italy.

. . . the word of the Lord came expressly
unto Ezekiel the priest, the son of Buzi,
in the land of the Chaldeans by the
river Chebar; and the hand of the Lord
was there upon him.

EZEKIEL 1:3

היה היה דבר־ה׳ אל־יחזקאל בן־בוזי
הכהן בארץ כשדים על־נהר כבר ותהי
עליו שם יד־ה׳.

יחזקאל א׳ ג

LVII. MICHELANGELO: *The Prophet Ezekiel;* Cappella Sistina, Vatican, Rome, Italy.

And the Lord shall roar from Zion,
And utter His voice from Jerusalem,
And the heavens and the earth shall
   shake;
But the Lord will be a refuge unto His
   people,
And a stronghold to the children of
   Israel.

                                    JOEL 4:16

וה׳ מציון ישאג ומירושלם יתן קולו
ורעשו שמים וארץ וה׳ מחסה לעמו
ומעוז לבני ישראל.

יואל ד׳טז

LVIII. MICHELANGELO: *The Prophet Joel;* Cappella Sistina, Vatican, Rome, Italy.

And the Lord spoke unto the fish, and
it vomited out Jonah upon the dry land.
JONAH 2:11

ויאמר ה׳ לדג ויקא את־יונה אל־היבשה·
יונה ב׳ יא

IONAS

LIX. JACOPO PALMA (The Younger): *The Prophet Jonah;* Chiesa Santa Maria della Salute,
  Venice, Italy.

And the word of the Lord came unto
Zechariah, saying: 'Thus hath the Lord
of hosts spoken, saying: Execute true
judgment, and show mercy and com-
passion every man to his brother; and
oppress not the widow, nor the father-
less, the stranger, nor the poor . . . '
ZECHARIAH 7:8-10

ויהי דבר־ה׳ אל־זכריה לאמר·   כה אמר
ה׳ צבאות לאמר משפט אמת שפטו
וחסד ורחמים עשו איש את־אחיו·
ואלמנה ויתום גר ועני · · ·
זכריה ז׳ ח־י

LX. MICHELANGELO: *The Prophet Zechariah;* Cappella Sistina, Vatican, Rome, Italy.

Now when Job's three friends heard of all this evil that was come upon him, they came every one from his own place, Eliphaz the Temanite, and Bildad the Shuhite, and Zophar the Naama-thite; and they made an appointment together to come to bemoan him and to comfort him.

JOB 2:11

וישמעו שלשת רעי איוב את כל־הרעה
הזאת הבאה עליו ויבאו איש ממקמו
אליפז התימני ובלדד השוחי וצופר
הנעמתי ויועדו יחדו לבוא לנוד־לו
ולנחמו׃

איוב ב' יא

LXI. JEAN FOUQUET: *Job and His Comforters;* Musée Condé, Chantilly, France.

Then said Boaz unto his servant that
was set over the reapers: 'Whose damsel is this?'

RUTH 2:5

ויאמר בעז לנערו הנצב על־הקוצרים למי
הנערה הזאת׃

רות ב׳ ה

LXII. NICOLAS POUSSIN: *Ruth and Boaz* (DETAIL); Louvre, Paris, France.

And the king loved Esther above all the
women, and she obtained grace and
favor in his sight more than all the vir-
gins; so that he set the royal crown upon
her head, and made her queen instead
of Vashti.

ESTHER 2:17

ויאהב המלך את־אסתר מכל־הנשים
ותשא־חן וחסד לפניו מכל־הבתולות
וישם כתר־מלכות בראשה וימליכה תחת
ושתי׃

מגלת אסתר ב׳ יז

LXIII. ANDREA DEL CASTAGNO: *Queen Esther;* Santa Apollonia, Florence, Italy.

... So Esther drew near, and touched the top of the scepter. Then said the king unto her: 'What wilt thou, queen Esther? for whatever thy request, even to the half of the kingdom, it shall be given thee.'

ESTHER 5:2-3

ותקרב אסתר ותגע בראש השרביט·
ויאמר לה המלך מה־לך אסתר המלכה
ומה־בקשתך עד־חצי המלכות וינתן לך·
מגלת אסתר ה׳ ב־ג

LXIV. JACOPO DEL SELLAJO: *Esther Appears before Ahasuerus;* Nationalmuseum, Budapest, Hungary.

Then took Haman the apparel and the
horse, and arrayed Mordecai, and
caused him to ride through the street
of the city, and proclaimed before him:
'Thus shall it be done unto the man
whom the king delighteth to honor.'
ESTHER 6:11

ויקח המן את־הלבוש ואת־הסוס וילבש
את־מרדכי וירכיבהו ברחוב העיר ויקרא
לפניו ככה יעשה לאיש אשר המלך חפץ
ביקרו.
מגלת אסתר ו׳ יא

LXV. PAOLO VERONESE: *Triumph of Mordecai;* Chiesa San Sebastiano, Venice, Italy.

In the same hour came forth fingers of a man's hand, and wrote over against the candlestick upon the plaster of the wall of the king's palace; and the king saw the palm of the hand that wrote. Then the king's countenance was changed in him, and his thoughts affrighted him . . .

DANIEL 5:5–6

בה־שעתא נפקו אצבען די יד־אנש וכתבן
לקבל נברשתא על־גירא די־כתל היכלא
די מלכא ומלכא חזה פס ידא די כתבה·
אדין ֗ מלכה זיוהי שנוהי ורעינהי
יבהלונה · · ·

דניאל ה׳ ה־ו

LXVI. MATTIA PRETI: *The Feast of Belshazzar;* Museo Nazionale, Naples, Italy.

Then the king commanded, and they
brought Daniel, and cast him into the
den of lions . . .

DANIEL 6:17

באדין מלכא אמר והיתיו לדניאל ורמו
לגבא די אריותא · · ·
דניאל ו׳ יז

LXVII. GIOVANNI LORENZO BERNINI: *Daniel in the Lion's Den;* Chiesa di Santa Maria
del Popolo, Rome, Italy.

. . . and I saw in the vision, and I was by
the stream Ulai. And I lifted up mine
eyes, and saw, and, behold, there stood
before the stream a ram which had two
horns; and the two horns were high,
but one was higher than the other, and
the higher came up last.

DANIEL 8:2–3

ואראה בחזון ואני הייתי על־אובל
אולי· ואשא עיני ואראה והנה איל
אחד עמד לפני האבל ולו קרנים
והקרנים גבהות והאחת גבהה מן־
השנית והגבהה עלה באחרנה·
דניאל ח׳ ב־ג

LXVIII. REMBRANDT: *The Vision of Daniel;* Kaiser Friedrich Museum, Berlin, Germany.

BIOGRAPHIES OF ARTISTS

whose works appear in this book

followed by partial listings of their
works on Old Testament subjects

BIOGRAPHIES OF ARTISTS

JACOPO BASSANO (1510–1592) Italian

The Italian school of genre painting owes its existence in part to this artist who was one of its principal founders. In Bassano's paintings of Biblical incidents the people portrayed are peasants and the feeling of their everyday life is incorporated into this Venetian artist's work. Bassano's style was originally derived from Titian's, but later became an independent expression. It is of interest to note that the great artist El Greco (Domenico Theotocopulos) worked for a while in the Bassano workshop.

The Burning Bush, Meeting of Jacob and Rachel, Jacob's Journey, Boaz and Ruth, Building of the Ark, Samson and the Philistines, The Garden of Eden.

BARTOLOMMEO BELLANO (1430–1492) Italian

Architect and sculptor from Padua. His services as an architect were requested by Pope Paul II for work in the Vatican. The bronze relief *Cain and Abel* reproduced in this volume is the first of a series of twenty-one, depicting Bible stories. Bellano probably worked on these reliefs between the years 1484 and 1488.

Abel's Death, Sacrifice of Isaac, Joseph Is Sold, Crossing of the Red Sea, Worship of the Golden Calf, Samson's Death, David and Goliath, Judgment of Solomon, Jonah and the Whale.

GIOVANNI LORENZO BERNINI (1598–1680) Italian

Architect and sculptor, one of the great masters of early baroque. As a portraitist he worked in marble and bronze. Executed countless commissions for the Papal Court. Was invited to submit plans for the restoration of the Louvre, but French artists interfered.

David, Habakuk.

HANS BOL (1534–c.1590) German

Member of a large, artistically inclined family. Hans Bol was a watercolorist and painter of miniatures. Some of his pupils achieved fame. The two watercolors reproduced in this book are from a series of nine that are now in the collection of the Dresden Picture Gallery.

SEBASTIEN BOURDON (1616–c.1673) French

After studying in Paris, Bourdon went to Rome where he lived for a number of years. There he associated with his famous compatriots Nicolas Poussin and Claude Lorrain. The art of these two masters and the Italian atmosphere are the chief components of Bourdon's work.

Noah's Sacrifice, Solomon Sacrificing to the Idols; many drawings illustrating Old Testament stories.

DIRK BOUTS (c.1410–1475) Flemish

One of the foremost old Flemish masters and portraitists. Famous for glowing depth and transparent clearness of coloring. His figures show great restraint. His most famous work is his altarpiece in the Church of St. Peter in Louvain of which one panel is reproduced in this volume.

Shower of Manna, Abraham before Melchizedek, Feeding of Elijah, The Story of Job.

JAN BRUEGHEL (1568-1625) Flemish

Youngest son of Pieter. Known as the "Velvet Brueghel," a reference to his technique. He studied in Antwerp and Italy, like his father before him. His contribution was to the field of landscape painting. He supplied the landscape backgrounds for many figure painters, a common practice at that time. His most important collaboration was with Rubens.

The Flood, Daniel in the Lion's Den, The Garden of Eden, Adam and Eve in Paradise.

PIETER BRUEGHEL, THE ELDER (c.1525-1569) Flemish

This famous Flemish painter, the student of Pieter Koeck van Aalst, was chiefly under the spell of the profound Hieronymus Bosch. His artistic fame covers a wide variety of subject matter, landscapes, genre and especially peasant scenes. There are many hidden allusions in his work, constituting an important source for the historians of sixteenth century culture. All of his creations were painted with realism, humor and keen observation. His drawings are ranked with the very best. He studied the Italian Renaissance masters in Italy. Brueghel resided in Brussels.

Job on His Dunghill.

MASTER BERTRAM VAN BYRDE (early XV cent.) German

Bertram van Byrde is one more name in the long list of important artists whose career and body of works are nearly unknown and are problems still facing art historians. Master Bertram was born in Minden and from there wandered to Hamburg in 1367. He is praised by his contemporaries. He seems to have made a pilgrimage to Rome between 1390 and 1410. His art reflects the style which flourished in Germany during the reign of Charles IV. His paintings exhibit a strong and architectural feeling. The scene reproduced in this volume is from Master Bertram's Grabanow Altarpiece, now in the Hamburg Kunsthalle.

Separation of Darkness and Light, Creation of the Beasts, Creation of Man, Creation of Woman, Sacrifice of Isaac, A Prophet, Daniel.

ANDREA DEL CASTAGNO (1390-1457) Italian

The story is told that a Medici once observed a young man drawing pictures of cattle on flat smooth stones in the field. The Medici took the youth to Florence so that he could study art. That youth was Andrea del Castagno. He was given the opportunity to study with Uccello and Pesellino and probably saw Masaccio at work, as well. His principal work is considered to be the equestrian figure of *Nicola di Tolentino,* now to be seen in the Cathedral in Florence. His works often show interesting innovations and realistic observations carried out in a firm style. Vasari, the biographer, accused Castagno of having killed a fellow artist named Domenico Veneziano. This has been proven a false accusation, as Veneziano survived Castagno by four years.

Isaiah, David, Queen Esther.

RAPHAELINO DEL COLLE (c.1490-c.1540) Italian

Pupil, and later collaborator, of Raphael, whence his name.

PIERO DI COSIMO (1462-1521) Italian

In 1482 the young Pietro di Lorenzo accompanied his teacher Cosimo Rosselli to Rome to assist him in decorating the Sistine Chapel. Later, he changed his name to Piero di Cosimo to honor his master. He is famous for his paintings of mythological subjects as well as for his works with a strictly religious content. In his later years Cosimo appears to have been influenced by Leonardo da Vinci. Art historians are now re-evaluating his secular paintings and his fascinating personality. Many of his works are full of complex mythological allusions. Cosimo was Andrea del Sarto's master.

LORENZO COSTA (1460-1535) Italian

Costa strongly influenced the Ferrarese and Bolognese schools of painting. His independent use of landscape was a significant aspect of his art and was used as a point of departure for later Italian artists interested in genre and scenic painting.

LUCAS CRANACH, THE ELDER (147)2-1553 German

The master of the Lutheran Reformation. In 1493 he accompanied Frederick the Wise to the Holy Land, returning with him two years later to Wittenberg where he conducted a workshop and twice served as burgomaster. In 1504 he became court painter to Frederick. He travelled to the Netherlands and painted the portraits of Charles V and Maximilian. He was a close friend and ardent follower of Martin Luther. The Reformation found vivid expression in his work. His paintings combine skill and descriptive detail with the lofty spirit of the humanistic period in which he and his learned friends lived. His compositions are dignified, but also include humorous passages.

> *Samson and Delilah, Creation of the Animals, The Garden of Eden, Jacob's Dream, The Fall of Man, Lot and His Daughters, Sacrifice of Isaac, Destruction of Pharaoh.*

ALBRECHT DÜRER (1471–1528) German

Dürer was born in Nürnberg, Germany, the son of a Hungarian goldsmith. After apprenticing for three years to a local artist he travelled to Venice. Upon his return to Germany he worked in the studio of Martin Schongauer in Colmar. Later, he practiced wood engraving in Basle. In 1494 he established himself as master in Nürnberg. His art is usually divided into three periods. The first, 1494–1505, reflects the influence of his teacher Schongauer and the Italian, Andrea Mantegna. Some strong portraits and woodcuts as well as his famous *Adoration of the Magi* belong to this period. His second, and most prolific, period was from 1507 to 1520. During his final phase, 1521–1528, he devoted himself chiefly to portrait painting, copper engravings and the pursuit of literary activities. In art he was the highest expression of early sixteenth century humanism north of the Alps.

> *Adam, Eve, Job and His Wife.*

JEAN FOUQUET (c.1415–c.1480) French

Fouquet is best known for his miniatures, the most famous being the forty illustrations he made for the *Book of the Hours,* now in the Chantilly Museum, and the eleven miniatures illustrating the French translation of Josephus' *History of the Jews,* now in the Bibliothèque Nationale, in Paris. His vivid portraits have also been recognized as outstanding works of art. Fouquet was court painter to Charles VII.

> *Paradise, Building of the Tower of Babel, Fall of Jericho, Building of the Temple, Israelites Battle the Canaanites.*

PIERO DELLA FRANCESCA (c.1420–1492) Italian

This Umbrian painter was one of the most influential artists and theorists of the Renaissance. His experiments and innovations in perspective, light, atmosphere and psychological emphasis make him a significant factor in Western art. His solemn, weighty and monumental style, full of captivating architectural and anatomical passages, found expression in oil paintings as well as frescoes. The detail reproduced in this book is taken from his most important fresco at the Church of San Francesco in Avezzo. He was also the author of a highly regarded *Treatise on Perspective.*

> *The Queen of Sheba Appears before Solomon.*

FRANS FRANCKEN, THE THIRD (1607–67) Flemish

Member of a family of Flemish painters, a follower of Rubens.

> *Moses Striking the Rock.*

LORENZO GHIBERTI (c.1378–1455) Italian

Ghiberti's father taught him goldsmithing and as a result, he became interested in sculpture. Ghiberti also studied painting and executed some frescoes in Rimini. His fame as a sculptor was already established when he won a competition which gave him the commission to make the bronze portals for the Baptistery in Florence. He spent twenty-one years (1403–1424) working on the great Northern Door. The Eastern Door was his next major task. Michelangelo regarded them fine enough to be the "gates of paradise." The panels reproduced in this book are from this series. His technique of alluding to deep space and giving a softness to the hard metal are the stamp of this great sculptor's art.

> *The Creation, The Life of Cain and Abel, The Life of Noah, The Life of Abraham, Sacrifice of Isaac, Moses Receiving the Tablets, Fall of Jericho, Solomon and the Queen of Sheba, A Prophet.*

GIORGIONE (c.1478–1510) Italian

Real name, Giorgio Barbarelli. With Titian, this Venetian artist studied with Bellini. Like Titian, he was a sensitive colorist and a superb craftsman of delicate taste. Unlike Titian who lived to be ninety-nine years old and has to his credit a great corpus of art works, Giorgione only lived to the age of thirty-two and produced very few paintings, of which not many survived. Controversies continue over attributions of paintings ascribed to Giorgione's hand and the mystery that surrounds him has made his works all the more attractive. His finest works are imbued with pastoral expression, filled with graceful figures. He painted religious and mythological subjects, portraits as well as frescoes. These frescoes, for the facades of Venetian palaces, have practically disappeared.

> *The Finding of Moses, The Ordeal of Moses, Jacob and Rachel, Moses and the Glowing Coals, David with the Head of Goliath.*

[167]

GIULIO ROMANO (1492–1546) Italian

This Umbrian artist became an assistant of Raphael when quite young and helped in the decoration of the Vatican. As Raphael's favorite pupil, he became his heir and art executor.

With Raphael and Penni: *Esau Seeks His Father's Blessing, Jacob's Meeting with Rachel, Joseph Interprets Pharaoh's Dream, Moses Saved from the Nile, Worship of the Golden Calf.* With Raphael: *Moses Drawing Water from the Rock.*

BENOZZO GOZZOLI (1420–1498) Italian

In Rome and Orvieto, Gozzoli was Fra Angelico's assistant, and his later work in Montefalco still shows Angelico's teachings. In 1456 Gozzoli returned to his native Florence, and there he painted one of his most important works, *The Journey of the Magi to Bethlehem.* His masterpiece is considered to be the cycle of twenty-four frescoes of Old Testament subjects painted in the Campo Santo in Pisa. Gozzoli's style is characterized by its charm, naturalness and decorative quality. All this is reinforced by the use of clear and bright colors which, unfortunately, have paid their tribute to the impact of time.

Noah's Vintage, Curse of Ham, The Flight of Lot, Rebecca and Eliezer, The Marriage of Jacob, Joseph and His Brothers, Joseph's Brothers Plot against Him, Joseph and the Wife of Potiphar, Moses and the Glowing Coals, The Fall of Jericho, Meeting of Solomon and the Queen of Sheba.

JUSTUS OF GHENT (middle XV century) Flemish

As yet, this artist's real name has not been identified although some scholars associate the name Joos van Wassenhove with him. It is thought that he was a pupil of the Van Eycks. His shadowy career can at least be traced to Italy where, for a while, he worked on a commission for Duke Frederico of Montefeltre and produced the only work that can with authenticity be ascribed to him.

GIOVANNI LANFRANCO (1581–1647) Italian

Lanfranco was a student of Agostino and Annibale Carracci. He executed Annibale's designs for the frescoes in the Farnese Palace. He also carried out a number of commissions for altarpieces in churches of Naples, Rome and elsewhere.

GREGORIO LAZZARINI (1657–1735) Italian

A leading member of the Venetian school. Giovanni Battista Tiepolo was among his many pupils. During his lifetime his contemporaries placed him on a level with Raphael.

Moses Striking the Rock, The Shower of Manna, Abraham's Sacrifice.

CLAUDE LORRAIN (1600–1682) French

This artist's real name was Gelée; he was called Lorrain, after the province where he was born. He studied in Rome, where he settled. His style combined the French feeling for nature with the Italian idea of classicism. He returned to France for a short while and painted the ceiling of the Carmelite Church in Nancy. His foremost patron in Rome was Pope Urban VIII. Lorrain is primarily known for his landscapes which have exerted a great influence on artists. He differs from his contemporary, Poussin, in his emphasis on the changing effects of light emanating from the horizon. His etchings are of a rare quality.

Hagar Driven out by Abraham, Hagar in the Desert, Marriage of Isaac and Rebecca, The Golden Calf, Embarkation of the Queen of Sheba.

BERNARDINO LUINI (1475–c.1533) Italian

At one time, certain gentle, attractive paintings were ascribed to Leonardo da Vinci. Later, it was learned that a student and artist named Luini, whose style was derived from Leonardo's, was responsible for those works. This Milanese artist had consciously developed a style of painting utilizing the serene grace for which Leonardo was famous. Some authorities note that Luini's early works have a freshness of conception and warmth in the harmony of colors which are less noticeable in his later work.

The Scorn of Cain, Death of the First-Born, Flight of the Jews from Egypt, Crossing of the Red Sea, Gathering of Manna, Moses on Mount Sinai, Miriam Rejoicing, Joseph and Potiphar's Wife.

MASACCIO (1401–c.1428) Italian

Masaccio died at the age of twenty-seven and yet his brief creative span changed the direction of Western art. It is significant that, despite his indifference to his personal appearance (the name Masaccio means "careless Thomas"), in his art his brilliant manipulation of form in light and color gave weight and monumentality to his subject. He achieved naturalistic effects through his knowledge of perspective and his ability to render true human emotions in form, color and movement. His greatest triumph became his frescoes in the Brancacci Chapel in Florence where the detail of *Adam and Eve* included in this volume is located.

The Fall of Man.

JAN MASSYS (c.1509–1575) Flemish

Son of the Antwerp master Quentin Massys (c.1466–1530), Jan painted religious and genre subjects in his father's style. One of his idiosyncracies was to repeat the same theme, giving each rendition a different interpretation. He would sign only the first of the series and therefrom stems some of the confusion concerning the extent of his works.

Lot and His Daughters, David and Bathsheba.

MICHELANGELO (1475–1564) Italian

No name is more familiar in the art world than that of Michelangelo Buonarrati who embodies the culmination of the Italian Renaissance. He was a painter, sculptor, architect and poet. While a student of the Ghirlandajo brothers, he exhibited a piece of sculpture in the Medici gardens of Florence which attracted the attention of the "magnificent" Lorenzo de Medici. Lorenzo took young Michelangelo into his household where the young artist had an opportunity to study ancient works of art and also see the best painting and sculpture of contemporary Florence. When Michelangelo was twenty-six he carved the statue of *David*, the city symbol of Florence. After a series of notable frescoes and sculptures Michelangelo went to Rome to decorate the Sistine Chapel. This monumental task took him four and a half years. His architectural accomplishments are considered as notable as his paintings and sculpture. He designed buildings, staircases, tombs. From 1534 until his death, Michelangelo lived in Rome serving various popes as chief sculptor, painter and architect for the Vatican. His final commission was the *Last Judgment* fresco in the Sistine Chapel. His *Moses* reveals the tragedy of Michelangelo's work, being conceived as one of forty-two statues for the tomb of Pope Julius II, which was never really completed. The famous figure of Moses became finally part of a setting which, though symbolically full of meaning, was but a shadow of the original plan. Michelangelo, through his preference for the human form, shows the fulfillment of the basic humanism in the Renaissance.

Panels of the vaults of the Sistine Chapel ceiling devoted to scenes from Genesis and paintings of the Prophets. Statues of Moses, David, Rachel, Leah.

PEDRO DE MOYA (1610–1666) Spanish

A pupil of Juan de Castillo. Out of a sense of adventure, he joined the army of Flanders. Enamored of the work of Van Dyck, he travelled to London to study under the master, returning home when Van Dyck died shortly afterward. He executed a series of paintings illustrating the life of Joseph, of which one is reproduced in this book.

Joseph and His Brothers, Joseph and the Wife of Potiphar.

JACOPO PALMA, THE YOUNGER (1544–1628) Italian

Named after his grandfather, he modelled his style after the latter's contemporaries, Titian and Tintoretto. An excellent example of his work is a painting in the Athenaeum in Helsinki, Finland, *The Prophet Elijah Carried up to Heaven*. He favored vivid colors, displayed in a facile technique.

Death of Abel, Triumph of David, Conversion of Saul.

FRANCESCO PESELLINO (1422–1457) Italian

Because of the brief span of this artist's life, Pesellino's works are rare. He served as apprentice to Fra Filippo Lippi. Paintings of animals and *cassoni* (decorative panels for chests) were Pesellino's specialties. His altarpiece in Pistoja is said to have been completed by Filippo Lippi after Pesellino's death.

Death of Absalom, Penitence of King David.

FRANCESCO POLAZZO (1683–1753) Italian

Pupil of Piazzetta whose influence can be traced in his use of color. Polazzo worked for the patricians of Venice, especially the Baglioni family. He is primarily known as a restorer of paintings.

NICOLAS POUSSIN (1594–1665) French

When Poussin was thirty he journeyed to Rome where he remained for six years. Some of his important paintings and his aesthetic formulations belong to this period. In 1640 he went to Paris, having been invited by Cardinal Richelieu to decorate a gallery of the Louvre. Intrigues and court exigencies which offended his artistic standards made him return to Rome in 1643. Here he spent his most productive and important period. Poussin's main contribution is his adaptation of the classic element to his art. This has exerted a serious influence on many artists. The perfect balance of his landscapes, in which he found the final solution for the effortless transition from foreground to background, secures his place in the history of art as the classic master of easel painting, and makes Cézanne's admiration for Poussin understandable.

> *Fratricide of Cain, Noah Builds an Altar, Moses Saved from the Water, The Israelites Offer Thanksgiving, Moses Striking Water from the Rock, The Golden Calf, David Vanquishes Goliath, Esther before Ahasuerus, Jonah Cast into the Sea.*

MATTIA PRETI (1613–1699) Italian

This artist who favored somber tones and scenes of death was commonly known as "Il Calabrese." Preti's reputation is based chiefly on his decorations of public buildings in Venice and Bologna, and his frescoes in the Cathedral in Malta. For this last commission he was knighted by Pope Urban VIII.

> *The Queen of Sheba Displays Her Gifts to King Solomon.*

RAPHAELO SANZIO (1483–1520) Italian

"Raphael," early in his life was exposed to high culture. Born to a poet-painter who was attached to the court of the Duke of Montefeltre, he was trained in the arts by his father and Timoteo Viti. At the age of sixteen he studied under the master artist Perugino, in Perugia. Raphael's early paintings of this Umbrian period display an independent spirit despite the strong association with his master. At the age of twenty-one Raphael went to Florence where he became interested in the scientific art problems of Leonardo and Michelangelo. His works became more subtly colored, technically perfect and space-conscious. In 1508 he joined Michelangelo, his former teacher Perugino and other prominent artists in the decoration of papal Rome. He took over the task of painting the frescoes for the Stanza della Segnatura in the Vatican. This room is considered by many experts to be a superb blending of architecture and decoration. Raphael, like many of his contemporary artists, was also an architect. His untimely death is one of the great tragedies in the history of the arts in Western civilization.

> *12 arcades of 4 Old Testament paintings each in the Loggia of the Vatican—commonly called "Raphael's Bible": Creation of the World, Adam and Eve; the stories of Noah, Abraham, Isaac, Jacob, Joseph, Moses, Joshua, David, Solomon, Esther.*

REMBRANDT VAN RIJN (1606–1669) Dutch

Through his paintings, drawings and etchings, Rembrandt's name has become a tradition, a synonym for art at its very best. By the age of twenty Rembrandt had developed a personal style and was painting important canvasses in the city of his birth, Leiden. By the time he moved to Amsterdam (1631) he was one of the leading artists of Holland. He painted with light and thought in color. His etchings are regarded as outstanding examples of graphic art. His portraits reveal sensitive character reading. Rich colors, broad brushwork, power of observation and technical skill characterize his best work. Rembrandt was a member of the Mennonite sect, a group which particularly revered the Old Testament. With this background, and the fact that there were many Jews in Amsterdam during the seventeenth century, it is not at all surprising that Rembrandt was closely associated with his Jewish neighbors, living in the Ghetto with them and frequently using them as modéls for his paintings.

> *Sacrifice of Abraham, Abraham and Hagar, Isaac Blessing Jacob, Jacob Wrestling with the Angel, Joseph's Dream, Joseph and Potiphar's Wife, Samson's Wedding Feast, The Writing on the Wall, Haman before Esther and Ahasuerus, Haman in Disgrace.*

PETER PAUL RUBENS (1577–1640) Flemish

After studying in Antwerp, Rubens went to Italy where his work attracted the attention of the Duke of Mantua who made him his court painter. One of Rubens' tasks was to copy the paintings of other masters for the Duke's private art collection. In 1608 he returned to Antwerp, called back to his mother's deathbed. One year later he became official painter of the court of Archduke Albert and renounced his intention of returning to Italy. Rubens was a rare combination of artist and statesman. In 1624 Philip IV of Spain vested him with a title and three years later he was sent to England with the rank of Ambassador to negotiate for peace between that country and Spain. Upon his return to Antwerp he resumed his artistic work. There are between two and three thousand paintings accredited to him, though a great number of them were actually executed by his pupils, after his design.

> *Adam and Eve in Paradise, Abraham and Melchizedek, The Repudiation of Hagar, Lot and His Daughters, Flight of Lot, Reconciliation of Esau and Jacob, King David and His Harp, Bathsheba, Samson and the Lion, Judgment of Solomon, Jonah Cast into the Sea, Esther before Ahasuerus.*

ANDREA DEL SARTO (1486–1531) Italian

So called because his father was a tailor; real name, Andrea d'Angelo di Francesco. Equally famous for his frescoes and oils, he has been called the "faultless painter." Del Sarto's work was primarily religious in theme and is distinguished for richness of color, precision of draftsmanship and monumental composition.

JACOPO DE SELLAJO (c.1441–c.1497) Italian

His paintings of mythological and Old Testament subjects, generally not well known, reveal strong reflections of the art of his teachers Botticelli and Filippino Lippi.

Creation of Adam and Eve, Coronation of Esther.

BERNARDO STROZZI (1581–1644) Italian

Strozzi was originally a Franciscan monk who deserted his order to become a secular priest. His preserved works in Venice and Genoa, oil paintings and frescoes, exhibit a vigorous temper in style and technique.

David with the Head of Goliath, Bathsheba and King David.

GIOVANNI BATTISTA TIEPOLO (1696?–1770) Italian

Tiepolo's earliest works are in Venice and in that general area. This illusionistic artist decorated ceilings and walls alike in a style originally derived from the work of Paolo Veronese. Tiepolo had an inventive mind and a personal style. In his mastery of the fresco technique he achieved a great number of remarkable works. There are also a few easel paintings by Tiepolo in which his true individuality is strikingly preserved.

Abraham's Vision, Hagar in the Wilderness, Finding of Moses, The Sacrifice of Isaac, Jacob's Dream, Joshua Holds Back the Sun, Rachel Hides the Idols, Judgment of Solomon, Elijah, Isaiah, Ezekiel.

TINTORETTO (1518–1594) Italian

This artist's real name was Jacopo Robusti. He acquired the name by which he is known in the art world because his father was a "tintore" (dyer). He was also known as "Il Furioso" because of his manner of working—with great speed and intensity. His work was chiefly done in Venice where he decorated the Academy, the Ducal Palace and numerous churches. Tintoretto's color and painting style in the treatment of light and shadow made him one of the outstanding Italian masters. His painting of *Paradise* in the Ducal Palace, Venice, is the largest canvas ever painted by a master artist (30 feet by 74 feet).

Adam and Eve, Paradise, Death of Abel, Sacrifice of Isaac, Joseph and Potiphar's Wife, Finding of Moses, Moses Striking the Rock, Solomon and the Queen of Sheba, Death of Samson, Joshua, Job, Jeremiah.

TITIAN (c.1477–1576) Italian

The word Titian has come to be identified with rich, transparent and subdued golden-red color tones. The real name of the artist with which it is associated was Tiziano Vecelli, a native of the colorful Dolomite Alps. In his youth Titian went to Venice where he studied under the superb tutelage of the master artist Bellini. He was a schoolmate and later a student of Giorgione. Titian succeeded Bellini as chief painter of Venice, working in the major churches and palaces of that city. Commissions for portraits took him to Bologna and Augsburg, bringing Titian in contact with many European nobles. He died of the plague at the age of ninety-nine.

Sacrifice of Isaac, David and Goliath, The Fall of Man, Cain Slays Abel.

PERINO DEL VAGA (1500–1547) Italian

Del Vaga worked chiefly in Rome and Genoa. In the former city he assisted Raphael in decorating the Loggia in the Vatican. He left Rome in 1527 and went to Genoa where he painted a series of historical and mythological frescoes for the Doria Palace which are considered his main works.

Creation of Eve, Crossing of the Red Sea (with Raphael).

PAOLO VERONESE (1528–1588) Italian

The name Veronese is derived from the artist's birthplace, Verona. His early works, frescoes and altarpieces, were painted in that city and in Mantua. About 1555 he moved to Venice where he became a leading figure in the world of art. His great cycle of frescoes in the church of San Sebastiano is a monument to his genius. He was primarily a decorative painter, subordinating psychological and spiritual emphasis to color, composition, sheer beauty and spectacle.

Cain and His Family, Finding of Moses, Hagar and the Angel, Rachel at the Well, Anointing of David, Lot and His Daughters, Sacrifice of Isaac, Esther, Bathsheba and David, Esther before Ahasuerus, Israelites Fleeing Egypt, Burning of Sodom, The Queen of Sheba before Solomon.

ANDREA DEL VERROCCHIO (1435–1488)
Italian

Florentine sculptor, silversmith, painter and engineer whose workshop was a training center for the young artists of Florence, foremost among them, Leonardo da Vinci. A conscientious but uninspired precisionist. Few of his paintings are left. He was most famous for his work in bronze.